Sanjeev Kapoor's KHAZANA

Chicken Recipes

In association with Alyona Kapoor

Popular Prakashan
www.popularprakashan.com

Published by
POPULAR PRAKASHAN PVT. LTD.
301, Mahalaxmi Chambers
22, Bhulabhai Desai Road
Mumbai - 400 026
for KHANA KHAZANA PUBLICATIONS PVT. LTD.

First Published 2007
Sixth Reprint 2014

(4070)
ISBN: 978-81-7991-322-2

Design: FourPlus Advertising Pvt. Ltd.

PRINTED IN INDIA by
Saurabh Printers Pvt. Ltd.
A-16, Sector 4, Noida

AUTHOR'S NOTE

Chicken, which was once served only at celebrations or as a Sunday treat, has now become a regular mealtime favourite. Today a non-vegetarian meal is considered incomplete without one or more chicken dishes on the menu.

One of the most versatile of all foods, chicken can be cooked in a variety of delicious ways. Tender grilled marinated chunks of chicken make for wonderful cocktail snacks, as do velvety seekh kebabs. Hearty chicken soups are celebrated the world over for their restorative properties, and chicken salads are a fixture on many a restaurant menu. The sight of a whole golden brown roasted chicken on a platter, or pieces of chicken smothered in a rich red creamy gravy can test the resolve of the most health-conscious diner, who will throw all caution to the winds before serving himself a hearty portion of the succulent bird.

In fact, dieters the world over choose chicken to indulge in guilt-free feasts of this high-protein food. Its lean, white meat is the preferred alternative to red meats. An added advantage is that the fat in chicken can be further reduced by about 10 grams per serving if the skin is removed before cooking!

In this book I have put together a range of recipes for every occasion and for every course in a meal. There are simple recipes like everyone's favourite Sweetcorn Chicken Soup as well as the more exotic Spaghetti With Chicken And Eggplant and Murgh Benarasi Beeda. Herb-Crusted Chicken With Peach Sauce will wow your guests at a special celebration, while Chicken Stew With Garlic Bread will provide you with comfort food at the end of a stressed-out day. There are recipes from across India - Kozhi Melagu Varuval of Chettinad fame, Kori Ajadina from Mangalore and the ubiquitous Tandoori Chicken with its dressed-up version, Butter Chicken.

Delicacies from across the continents are featured including Kung Pao Chicken, Stuffed Roast Chicken and Thai Chicken and Noodle Soup. As always, every recipe serves four persons, and has been tried, tested and presented in easy-to-follow steps.

A few words of caution on the safe-handling of chicken:

- Buy freshly processed chicken - check the date if purchasing a packaged bird.
- Wrap chicken well before freezing to avoid freezer burn - dark, leathery spots on the surface caused by exposure to cold air.

- Prevent "cross-contamination" by keeping fresh chicken separate from other foods. Place raw chicken in a plastic bag so juices won't drip onto other foods.

- Chicken should be defrosted in the refrigerator, in cold water or in a microwave oven. The best method of defrosting is to slowly thaw the chicken in the refrigerator.

- Defrost chicken in cold water in its airtight packaging or in a leak-proof bag. Submerge the whole bird or cut-up parts in cold water, changing the water every 30 minutes to be sure it stays cold.

- Chicken defrosted in the microwave should be cooked immediately after thawing because some areas of the food may become warm and begin to cook during microwaving.

- Always wash utensils that have touched raw chicken with hot, soapy water before using them for the cooked chicken. Wash counters, cutting boards and other surfaces raw chicken has touched to prevent contamination.

Happy Cooking!

CONTENTS

MAIN COURSE - INDIAN

MAIN COURSE - INTERNATIONAL

SWEETCORN CHICKEN SOUP

Ingredients

- ½ cup sweetcorn kernels
- 150 grams cream-style sweetcorn
- 1 boneless chicken breast, boiled and shredded
- 3 tablespoons cornflour
- 2 tablespoons oil
- 1 tablespoon cabbage, chopped
- ¼ medium carrot, diced
- 4-5 cups Chicken Stock (page 10)
- salt to taste
- ¼ teaspoon white pepper powder
- ½ tablespoon sugar
- ¼ teaspoon MSG (optional)
- 1 stalk spring onion greens, chopped

Method

1 Mix cornflour with half a cup of water and set aside.

2 Heat oil in a wok or pan; add cabbage, carrot and corn kernels and stir-fry for a couple of minutes. Add chicken and stir-fry for a couple of minutes more.

3 Stir in the chicken stock and bring the mixture to a boil.

4 Mix in the cream-style sweetcorn and continue cooking for two to three minutes.

5 Add salt, white pepper powder, sugar and MSG. Stir in the cornflour mixture and cook on high heat for one minute or until the soup thickens, stirring continuously.

6 Serve piping hot, garnished with the chopped spring onion greens.

CHICKEN STOCK

Boil 200 grams chicken bones in water for 5 minutes. Drain and discard water.

Boil blanched bones with a roughly chopped carrot, celery stalk, leek, 2-3 parsley stalks, 6-7 black peppercorns, 5-6 cloves, 1 bay leaf and 10 cups of water.

Remove any scum which rises to the surface and replace it with more cold water. Simmer the stock for at least one hour.

Remove from heat, strain, cool and store in a refrigerator till further use.

THAI CHICKEN AND NOODLE SOUP

Ingredients

- 2 (175 grams each) boneless chicken breasts
- 1 cup thread egg noodles, broken into small pieces
- 1 tablespoon oil
- 3-4 garlic cloves
- 1 spring onion, chopped
- 4 cups Chicken Stock (page 10)
- 1 teaspoon crunchy peanut butter
- 1-inch ginger, sliced
- salt to taste
- 1 tablespoon fresh coriander leaves, chopped
- 2 fresh red chillies, slit
- ½ tablespoon lemon juice
- ¼ cup thick coconut milk

Method

1. Remove skin and cut chicken into fine pieces.

2. Heat oil in a deep pan; add garlic and spring onion, and sauté for one minute on medium heat until light golden brown.

3. Add chicken stock, peanut butter, ginger and chicken; bring the mixture to a boil.

4. When the chicken is cooked, add salt, coriander leaves, fresh red chillies and lemon juice. Bring to a boil again.

5. Stir in egg noodles and coconut milk, and immediately take the pan off the heat.

6. Cover and leave to stand for two minutes. Serve hot.

SICHUAN CHICKEN SOUP

Ingredients

100 grams boneless chicken

2 spring onions

1 small carrot, grated

¼ small cabbage, shredded

4 dried black mushrooms, chopped

½ medium capsicum, chopped

4-5 French beans, chopped

50 grams bean curd (tofu), cut into ½-inch squares

3 tablespoons cornflour

1 teaspoon salt

3 tablespoons vinegar

1 teaspoon sugar

1 tablespoon red chilli paste

6-8 white peppercorns, crushed

3 cups Chicken Stock (page 10)

Method

1 Clean, wash and cut chicken into very small pieces.

2 Finely chop spring onion bulbs and three or four green stalks.

3 Mix the cornflour with a quarter cup of water; stir in salt, vinegar, sugar, red chilli paste and crushed peppercorns.

4 Put the carrot, cabbage, spring onion bulb, mushrooms, capsicum, French beans, chicken, and chicken stock into a deep microwave-safe bowl. Cover and cook on HIGH (100%) for eight minutes.

5 Add the cornflour mixture and bean curd and cook, uncovered, on HIGH (100%) for five minutes.

6 Serve piping hot, garnished with spring onion greens.

TROPICAL CHICKEN AND FARFALLE SALAD

Ingredients

- 200 grams boneless chicken, boiled and shredded
- 1 cup farfalle (bow-tie pasta)
- 1 medium tomato, cut into ½-inch cubes
- 1 medium carrot, cut into ½-inch cubes
- ½ medium green capsicum, cut into ½-inch cubes
- ½ medium yellow capsicum, cut into ½-inch cubes (optional)
- 8-10 olives, sliced into rings

Dressing

- 4-5 garlic cloves, chopped
- 2 inches celery stalk, finely chopped
- ½ teaspoon crushed red chillies
- 2-3 tablespoons lemon juice
- salt to taste
- 2 teaspoons finely chopped fresh parsley

Method

1 Boil three cups of water in a deep pan. Add pasta and cook till just done (al dente). Drain and set aside to cool.

2 To make the dressing, combine garlic, celery, red chillies, lemon juice, salt and parsley in a bowl.

3 In a separate bowl, combine pasta, chicken, tomato, carrot, green and yellow capsicums and olives.

4 Pour the dressing over and toss to mix. Serve immediately.

CHEF'S TIP

Pasta is cooked to perfection when it is "al dente" - cooked but still firm to the bite.

AVOCADO AND CHICKEN SALAD

Ingredients

1 medium avocado

1 (150 grams) boneless chicken breast, boiled and thinly sliced

½ head iceberg lettuce

2 celery stalks, thinly sliced

2 eggs, boiled and sliced

1 medium tomato, sliced

Dressing

4 tablespoons cheese spread

white pepper powder to taste

4 tablespoons fresh cream

2 tablespoons fresh parsley, chopped

6-8 garlic cloves, chopped

salt to taste

Method

1 Peel, and halve the avocado; remove seed and cut the flesh into thin slices.

2 For the dressing, mix cheese spread, white pepper powder, fresh cream, parsley, garlic and salt.

3 Arrange chicken slices, avocado slices, celery, egg slices and tomato slices in a pattern on a bed of lettuce.

4 Pour the dressing over the salad and serve immediately.

TANDOORI MURGH CHAAT

Ingredients

- 2 (150 grams each) boneless chicken breasts, skin removed
- 1 teaspoon Kashmiri chilli powder
- 1 teaspoon ginger paste
- 1 teaspoon garlic paste
- ½ cup drained yogurt
- salt to taste
- 1 tablespoon lemon juice
- ½ teaspoon *garam masala* powder
- 2 teaspoons mustard oil
- 2 tablespoons butter
- 1 small green capsicum, cut into thin strips
- ½ each small red and yellow capsicums, cut into thin strips
- 1 medium onion, sliced
- 2 green chillies, chopped
- 2 tablespoons fresh coriander leaves, chopped
- 1 tablespoon lemon juice
- 1 teaspoon *chaat masala*
- ½ small unripe green mango (optional), chopped
- salt to taste

Method

1 Make incisions with a sharp knife on the chicken breasts and set aside.

2 Combine chilli powder, ginger paste, garlic paste, drained yogurt, salt, lemon juice, *garam masala* powder and mustard oil. Spread this mixture over the chicken breasts and leave to marinate for three to four hours, preferably in a refrigerator.

3 Preheat the oven to 200°C. Thread the chicken onto skewers and cook for ten to twelve minutes, or until almost tender. Baste chicken with butter and cook for another four minutes.

4 Remove from heat and shred chicken when cool.

5 In a large bowl, combine shredded chicken, green, red and yellow capsicums, onion, green chillies, half the coriander leaves, lemon juice, *chaat masala*, green mango and salt. Toss well to mix.

6 Transfer to a serving plate and serve, garnished with the remaining fresh coriander leaves.

CHICKEN SATAY

Ingredients

4 (150 grams each) chicken breasts, skin removed

2 tablespoons lemon juice

1 tablespoon dark soy sauce

1 teaspoon oil

1 teaspoon red chilli powder

salt to taste

Peanut Sauce

1 teaspoon oil

1 small onion, grated

4 garlic cloves, chopped

½ teaspoon red chilli powder

1 tablespoon dark soy sauce

3 tablespoons tomato purée

2 teaspoons honey

¼ cup roasted peanuts, coarsely crushed

salt to taste

Method

1 Soak wooden skewers (satay sticks) in water for at least half an hour.

2 Cut each chicken breast into half-inch broad strips and flatten lightly.

3 Mix lemon juice, soy sauce, oil, chilli powder and salt in a bowl. Mix in the chicken and set aside to marinate for one hour.

4 Thread chicken onto the wooden skewers.

5 Heat a non-stick flat *tawa*, grease it lightly with a few drops of oil and place a few skewers with the chicken on it. Cook on high heat, turning frequently, for three to four minutes, or till just cooked.

6 Alternatively, cook chicken in a preheated grill for ten to twelve minutes or until done, turning skewers a couple of times.

7 For the peanut sauce, heat oil in a pan; add grated onion and chopped garlic and cook on high heat, stirring continuously, for half a minute.

8 Add chilli powder, soy sauce, tomato purée, honey, crushed peanuts, salt and one cup of water.

9 Bring the sauce to a boil and simmer for five minutes, stirring occasionally.

10 Serve the chicken satay with peanut sauce.

DAHI MURGH KEBAB

Ingredients

600 grams chicken mince (*keema*)

¼ cup split Bengal gram (*chana dal*)

2 tablespoons oil + for deep-frying

1 teaspoon cumin seeds

1 teaspoon coriander seeds

5-6 black peppercorns

2 black cardamoms

1½ inches ginger, chopped

10 garlic cloves, chopped

salt to taste

2 teaspoons red chilli powder

½ teaspoon green cardamom powder

a pinch of mace (*javitri*) powder

½ teaspoon *garam masala* powder

2 eggs, beaten

Stuffing

1 small onion, finely chopped

¼ cup drained yogurt

2 teaspoons fresh mint leaves, chopped

salt to taste

Method

1 Soak *chana dal* in two cups of water for at least three hours. Drain.

2 For the stuffing, squeeze the chopped onion between your palms to remove excess water. In a bowl mix drained yogurt, chopped onion, chopped mint leaves and salt. Divide into sixteen equal portions, cover and place in a refrigerator.

3 Heat two tablespoons of oil in a pan; add cumin seeds, coriander seeds, peppercorns, black cardamom seeds, ginger and garlic and stir-fry for one minute on medium heat. Add chicken mince and sauté for five minutes.

4 Add soaked *chana dal*, salt, chilli powder, cardamom powder, mace powder and *garam masala* powder. Stir well for two minutes.

5 Add one-and-a-half cups of water and bring the mixture to a boil. Lower heat and cook, covered, till *chana dal* is completely cooked. Cook on high heat to dry out the mixture completely, stirring continuously. Remove from heat and set aside to cool.

6 Grind chicken and *chana dal* mixture till smooth.

7 Divide chicken mixture into sixteen equal portions. Flatten each portion in the palm of your hand and place a portion of onion and yogurt stuffing in the centre. Shape into round *tikkis* and flatten slightly.

8 Heat oil in a *kadai*. Dip each *tikki* in the beaten egg and deep-fry in hot oil till golden brown. Drain on absorbent paper.

9 Serve hot with onion *lachcha* and *pudina chutney*.

CHEF'S TIP

Moisten your palms to prevent the mixture from sticking while shaping the tikkis.

CHICKEN MAKHMALI KEBAB

Ingredients

- 4 (200 grams each) chicken breasts
- 4-6 green chillies, chopped
- 1 inch ginger, roughly chopped
- 5-6 garlic cloves, roughly chopped
- 2/3 cup yogurt
- 1/4 cup grated processed cheese
- 1/4 cup fresh cream
- 1/2 teaspoon nutmeg powder
- 2 teaspoons *garam masala* powder
- 1 tablespoon honey
- 1/2 tablespoon lemon juice
- salt to taste
- 1/4 cup butter

Method

1 Remove skin and bone and cut each chicken breast into two. Grind green chillies, ginger and garlic to a smooth paste. Rub the paste into the chicken, cover and set aside for fifteen minutes.

2 Tie yogurt up in a piece of muslin and set aside for half an hour to drain.

3 In a bowl, whisk drained yogurt, cheese, cream, nutmeg powder, *garam masala* powder, honey, lemon juice and salt to taste. Marinate chicken in this mixture for three hours in a refrigerator.

4 Place chicken pieces, an inch apart, on a wire rack.

5 Cook chicken in a Grill TOP and BOTTOM for twenty minutes, brushing with butter every five minutes.

6 Serve hot with *chutney*.

CHEF'S TIP

Use supremes of chicken for tender succulent kebabs.

MURGH KE WADE

Ingredients

- 100 grams chicken mince (*keema*)
- ¼ cup split hulled black gram (*dhuli urad dal*), soaked
- 2 green chillies, chopped
- 5 curry leaves
- salt to taste
- ½ teaspoon cumin seeds
- oil for deep-frying

Method

1 Wash and soak *urad dal* for three to four hours.

2 Drain and grind the *dal* with a very little water. Add green chillies and curry leaves and grind again.

3 Add chicken mince, salt, and cumin seeds and grind once more. Transfer the mixture to a bowl.

4 Heat oil in a *kadai*. Shape the chicken mixture with moistened hands into small balls and deep-fry till golden brown. Drain on absorbent paper. Serve hot.

KHAAS SEEKH

Ingredients

- 600 grams chicken mince (*keema*)
- 1 cup grated cottage cheese (*paneer*)
- ½ cup grated processed cheese
- 1½ teaspoons green cardamom powder
- 1 tablespoon *garam masala* powder
- 1 tablespoon fresh mint leaves, chopped
- ½ cup grated *khoya*/*mawa*
- 1 egg, beaten
- salt to taste
- 1 teaspoon white pepper powder
- oil for shallow-frying
- 1 teaspoon *chaat masala*

Method

1 Soak wooden skewers (satay sticks) in water for at least fifteen minutes.

2 Mix grated *paneer*, processed cheese, half the cardamom powder, half the *garam masala* powder and mint leaves in a bowl. Press a portion of the mixture around the skewer in a thin layer. Press the ends firmly.

3 In another bowl, mix grated *khoya* and chicken *keema*. Add beaten egg, salt, remaining cardamom powder, white pepper powder and remaining *garam masala* powder; mix well.

4 Press a portion of this mixture over the *paneer* mixture on the skewer. Refrigerate the *seekhs* for a while before frying.

5 Heat oil in a pan and shallow-fry the seekhs, turning to cook evenly on all sides.

6 Serve hot, sprinkled with *chaat masala*.

CHEF'S TIP

The wooden skewers are soaked in water to prevent them from burning while cooking. This is particularly necessary while grilling or cooking over an open flame.

KOMBDI PULAVA KEBAB

Ingredients

- 4 (150 grams each) boneless chicken breasts
- 1 tablespoon coriander seeds
- 2 green cardamoms
- ½ inch cinnamon
- 2 cloves
- 1 large onion
- 1/8 cup almonds, blanched and ground
- ¼ cup yogurt
- ¼ tablespoon black peppercorns, crushed
- ½ tablespoon ginger paste
- ¼ tablespoon garlic paste
- salt to taste
- black salt to taste
- *ghee* for shallow-frying
- 2 lemons, cut into wedges

Method

1 Soak wooden skewers (satay sticks) in water for at least fifteen minutes.

2 Preheat the oven to 180°C.

3 Heat a *tawa* and dry-roast coriander seeds, cardamoms, cinnamon and cloves, separately. Grind the spices to a powder.

4 Slit the chicken breasts into two and then into strips. Thread them onto the wooden skewers.

5 Roast the onion in the oven for thirty to forty minutes.

6 Combine the roasted onion, ground almonds, yogurt, crushed peppercorns, ginger paste, garlic paste, salt and black salt. Add the roasted spice powder and mix well.

7 Add the mixture to the skewered chicken and set aside to marinate for half an hour.

8 Heat some *ghee* on a *tawa* till very hot. Place the chicken on it and cook on high heat for two minutes. Lower heat and cook, turning the skewers a couple of times, till the *kebabs* are golden brown on both sides. Drizzle a little more *ghee* over the *kebabs* if necessary

9 Alternatively, cook the chicken in a preheated oven or *tandoor*. Serve hot with lemon wedges.

KEBAB KOMBDYACHE

Ingredients

- 4 (100 grams each) boneless chicken breasts
- salt to taste
- 2 tablespoons oil
- 4 medium onions, sliced
- 10 black peppercorns
- 1 tablespoon coriander seeds
- 1 inch cinnamon
- 3-4 cloves
- 3-4 green cardamoms
- 1 cup drained yogurt
- 1 tablespoon ginger paste
- ¼ cup cream
- 2 tablespoons oil
- a pinch of crushed black peppercorns
- 1 tablespoon lemon juice

Method

1 Soak wooden skewers (satay sticks) in water for at least fifteen minutes.

2 Clean, wash and cut chicken breasts into three lengthways. Mix in salt and set aside.

3 Heat oil in a *kadai* and sauté the onions till brown. Cool and grind onions to a fine paste.

4 Dry-roast peppercorns, coriander seeds, cinnamon, cloves and cardamoms. Grind the roasted spices to a fine powder.

5 Combine the browned onion paste, roasted spice powder, drained yogurt, ginger paste, cream and salt. Add the chicken and set aside to marinate for two hours, preferably in a refrigerator.

6 Thread the chicken pieces onto the wooden sticks and sprinkle crushed black peppercorns over the chicken.

7 Arrange the sticks on the barbecue or grill and cook, basting with oil every now and then and turning the sticks so that the chicken cooks evenly on all sides. Sprinkle with lemon juice.

8 Alternatively, place the sticks on a greased *tawa* and cook over a gas flame till done. Sprinkle with lemon juice, cover and cook till tender.

9 Transfer to a serving plate and serve hot.

CHICKEN SAUSAGE ROLLS

Ingredients

4 hot dog rolls

4 chicken sausages

2 tablespoons oil

1 head lettuce, shredded

2 medium onions, chopped

4 tablespoons tomato ketchup

2 teaspoons English mustard paste

1 jalapeño pepper, chopped

Method

1 Heat a *tawa* and a frying pan. Slit the hot dog rolls without cutting through and toast them lightly on the *tawa*.

2 Heat oil in the frying pan; add the sausages and sauté till golden brown on all sides.

3 Place some lettuce in each hot dog roll. Add a sausage and top with onions, tomato ketchup, mustard paste and jalapeño pepper. Serve immediately.

DRUMS OF HEAVEN

Ingredients

24 chicken wings
4-6 garlic cloves, ground to a paste
2 teaspoons red chilli paste
1 teaspoon soy sauce
1 teaspoon vinegar
½ teaspoon white pepper powder
¼ teaspoon MSG (optional)
salt to taste
¾ cup refined flour (*maida*)
¾ cup cornflour
2 eggs
6 tablespoons oil + for deep-frying

Method

1 Cut off wing tip, remove thin bone and pull the flesh to one end of the thick bone of each chicken wing.

2 Mix garlic paste, one teaspoon of red chilli paste, soy sauce, vinegar, white pepper powder, MSG and salt to taste. Marinate the chicken wings in this mixture for two hours, preferably in the refrigerator.

3 Mix refined flour, cornflour, eggs, salt, six tablespoons of oil, remaining red chilli paste and some water if required. Whisk thoroughly to make a thick batter of pouring consistency. Rest the batter for fifteen to twenty minutes.

4 Heat oil in a wok; dip the marinated wings in the batter and deep-fry on medium heat for three to four minutes, or until crisp and golden brown.

5 Drain on absorbent paper and serve hot with Sichuan sauce.

CHEF'S TIP

Chicken wings shaped into "lollipops", are available in supermarkets. Your butcher will also make them for you.

LAZIZ TIKKA MASALA

Ingredients

Chicken Tikkas

800 grams boneless chicken, cut into 1½-inch pieces

1 teaspoon Kashmiri chilli powder

1 tablespoon lemon juice

salt to taste

4 tablespoons oil

Marinade

1 cup drained yogurt

1 tablespoon ginger paste

1 tablespoon garlic paste

1 teaspoon Kashmiri chilli powder

1 teaspoon *garam masala* powder

1 tablespoon lemon juice

salt to taste

2 tablespoons mustard oil

Onion-Tomato Masala

3 medium onions, chopped

4 medium tomatoes, finely chopped

3 tablespoons oil

½ teaspoon cumin seeds

7-8 garlic cloves, finely chopped

1 teaspoon ginger paste

1 teaspoon garlic paste

½ teaspoon cumin powder

1½ teaspoons coriander powder

salt to taste

Gravy

2 tablespoons butter

1 teaspoon ginger paste

1 teaspoon garlic paste

¼ cup tomato purée

1 cup onion-tomato *masala*

1 teaspoon Kashmiri chilli powder

½ teaspoon *garam masala* powder

¼ small bunch fresh coriander leaves, chopped

1 teaspoon dried fenugreek leaves (*kasoori methi*), roasted

¼ cup fresh cream

1 inch ginger, cut into thin strips

Method

1 Mix red chilli powder, lemon juice and salt in a large bowl. Add chicken and marinate for about thirty minutes.

2 Combine the ingredients for the marinade and the marinated chicken. Marinate chicken for about three hours in the refrigerator.

3 Thread the chicken onto skewers. Heat oil on a *tawa* and place the skewers on it. Cook chicken, turning the skewers a few times, so that the chicken cooks and browns evenly on all sides. Take the pieces off the skewers and set aside.

4 For the onion-tomato *masala*, heat oil in a pan. Add cumin seeds, and when they begin to change colour, add onions and sauté till well browned.

5 Add finely chopped garlic and sauté till lightly browned. Add ginger paste, garlic paste and continue to sauté. Add cumin powder and coriander powder and mix well.

6 Add chopped tomato and cook on low heat till the tomatoes are completely cooked and the oil begins to separate. Add salt to taste.

7 For the gravy, heat butter in a separate pan; add ginger paste, garlic paste and tomato purée and sauté for two minutes. Add half a cup of water and cook for two to three minutes.

8 Add the chicken and onion-tomato *masala* and simmer till the gravy reduces a little. Add red chilli powder, *garam masala* powder and half the coriander leaves and cook for two minutes.

9 Add roasted *kasoori methi* powder and fresh cream and mix well. Take the pan off the heat, and serve hot, garnished with ginger strips and the remaining coriander leaves.

CHEF'S TIP

To drain yogurt, tie it up in a piece of muslin and place over a bowl for at least fifteen minutes.

CHANDI KORMA

Ingredients

1 whole chicken (1 kilogram), cut into 12 pieces

30 almonds

10-12 pistachios

3 tablespoons melon (*kharbooja*) seeds

1 teaspoon + 1 tablespoon rose petals

1 tablespoon garlic paste

1 tablespoon ginger paste

1 cup yogurt

salt to taste

1 teaspoon white pepper powder

½ teaspoon green cardamom powder

¼ cup *ghee*

3 medium onions, chopped

2-3 green chillies, crushed

½ cup *khoya/mawa*, grated

4 tablespoons fresh cream

a few drops of rose water

silver *varq*, to garnish

Method

1 Blanch almonds; peel and grind twenty almonds to a fine paste and cut the rest into slivers. Blanch and cut pistachios into slivers. Soak melon seeds in half a cup of warm water. Drain and grind seeds to a fine paste. Crush one teaspoon of rose petals.

2 In a bowl, combine chicken, garlic paste, ginger paste, yogurt, salt, white pepper powder, cardamom powder and crushed rose petals.

3 Heat *ghee* in a pan, add onion and sauté till translucent. Add green chillies and *khoya* and sauté for a few minutes.

4 Add melon seed paste and almond paste and continue to sauté.

5 Add marinated chicken and sauté for a few minutes. Lower heat and simmer till almost done.

6 Stir in half the slivered almonds and pistachios and half a tablespoon of rose petals. Cover and cook on low heat for ten minutes. Stir in the fresh cream and rose water.

7 To serve, arrange the chicken pieces on a serving plate and pour the gravy over. Cover with the silver *varq* and garnish with the remaining rose petals and slivers of almonds and pistachios.

CHICKEN CHETTINAD

Ingredients

- 1 whole chicken (1 kilogram), cut into 12 pieces
- 6-8 dried red chillies
- ½ fresh coconut, grated
- 2 teaspoons poppy seeds (*khuskhus*)
- 1 teaspoon coriander seeds
- ½ teaspoon cumin seeds
- 3 green cardamoms
- 2 cloves
- 1 inch cinnamon
- ½ star anise (*chakri phool/badiyan*)
- 1 teaspoon fennel seeds (*saunf*)
- 2 teaspoons ginger, chopped
- 2 teaspoons garlic, chopped
- ½ cup oil
- 1 large onion, chopped
- 10-12 curry leaves
- 3 medium tomatoes, chopped
- 1 teaspoon red chilli powder
- ½ teaspoon turmeric powder
- salt to taste
- 1 tablespoon lemon juice
- a few sprigs of fresh coriander leaves

Method

1 Sauté the red chillies, grated coconut, poppy seeds, coriander seeds, cumin seeds, cardamoms, cloves, cinnamon, star anise and fennel seeds separately in a little oil; grind sautéed spices with ginger and garlic to a paste.

2 Heat oil in a *degchi* and fry onions till golden. Add curry leaves and the ground paste and sauté for a few minutes. Add the tomatoes, red chilli powder, turmeric powder and salt.

3 Add chicken and mix well. Cook for five minutes, add two cups of water and lemon juice; cover and cook till the chicken is tender.

4 Garnish with coriander leaves and serve hot with boiled rice or *paranthas*.

CHEF'S TIP

Try this dish without the coconut for a different flavour.

KORI AJADINA

Ingredients

1 whole chicken (1 kilogram), cut into 1-inch pieces

2 tablespoons lemon juice

salt to taste

3 tablespoons oil

1 inch cinnamon

4-5 cloves

3-4 black peppercorns

1 bay leaf

10 curry leaves

1 inch ginger, finely chopped

5-6 garlic cloves, finely chopped

2 medium onions, finely chopped

1 cup grated fresh coconut

¼ small bunch fresh coriander leaves, finely chopped

3 medium tomatoes, finely chopped

Masala Powder

1 inch cinnamon

3 cloves

1-2 green cardamoms

4-5 black peppercorns

1 teaspoon poppy seeds (*khuskhus*)

1 teaspoon cumin seeds

1 tablespoon coriander seeds

½ teaspoon fenugreek seeds (*methi dana*)

6 Kashmiri chillies

5 Madras chillies

½ teaspoon turmeric powder

Method

1 Marinate chicken in lemon juice and salt for half an hour, preferably in the refrigerator.

2 Dry-roast all the ingredients for the *masala* powder. Cool and grind to a powder.

3 Heat oil in a *kadai*. Add cinnamon, cloves, peppercorns and bay leaf and sauté for half a minute; add curry leaves.

4 Add ginger and garlic and sauté for a couple of minutes. Add onions, stir well and sauté till golden brown.

5 Add ground *masala* powder, grated coconut and half the chopped

coriander leaves and cook for five minutes till fragrant.

6 Add tomatoes, stir well and cook for five minutes till tomatoes are soft.

7 Add marinated chicken and half a cup of water, stir to mix, cover and cook for ten minutes, or till the chicken is tender.

8 Remove from heat and garnish with the remaining coriander leaves. Serve hot.

CHEF'S TIP

This Mangalorean speciality goes well with neer dosa, roti or rice.

TANDOORI CHICKEN

Ingredients

1 whole chicken (800 grams)

1 teaspoon Kashmiri chilli powder

1 tablespoon lemon juice

salt to taste

Marinade

1 cup yogurt

1 teaspoon Kashmiri chilli powder

salt to taste

2 tablespoons ginger paste

2 tablespoons garlic paste

2 tablespoons lemon juice

½ teaspoon *garam masala* powder

2 tablespoons mustard oil

2 tablespoons butter for basting

½ teaspoon *chaat masala*

onion rings and lemon slices, to garnish

Method

1 Make incisions with a sharp knife on the chicken breast, legs and thighs.

2 Apply a mixture of the Kashmiri chilli powder, lemon juice and salt over the chicken and set aside for half an hour.

3 For the marinade, tie the yogurt up in a piece of muslin and drain over a bowl for fifteen to twenty minutes. Add the chilli powder, salt, ginger and garlic pastes, lemon juice, *garam masala* powder and mustard oil to the drained yogurt.

4 Rub the mixture over the chicken and marinate for three to four hours in a refrigerator.

5 Thread the chicken onto a skewer and cook in a moderately hot tandoor or a preheated oven (200°C) for ten to twelve minutes, or until almost done. Baste chicken with butter and cook for another four minutes. Remove and set aside.

6 Sprinkle *chaat masala* powder and serve with onion rings and lemon slices.

CHEF'S TIP

To make Chicken Tikka, use boneless chicken cut into one-and-a-half-inch cubes, and cook as above.

KAIRI MURGH

Ingredients

- 1 whole chicken (1 kilogram), cut into 1½-inch pieces
- 2 medium unripe green mangoes
- ½ tablespoon ginger paste
- ½ tablespoon garlic paste
- salt to taste
- 2 teaspoons *garam masala* powder
- ½ tablespoon green chilli paste
- 4-5 cloves
- 3 tablespoons oil
- 2 medium onions, finely sliced
- ¼ teaspoon turmeric powder
- 1½ teaspoons red chilli powder
- 2 teaspoons coriander powder
- 2 tablespoons fresh coriander leaves, chopped

Method

1 Peel and cut green mangoes into small pieces. Purée half the pieces.

2 In a bowl, mix the chicken with half the ginger paste, half the garlic paste, salt, half the *garam masala* powder, half the green chilli paste and puréed mango. Marinate for about an hour, preferably in the refrigerator.

3 Place a piece of coal over a gas flame till red hot. Put it into a *katori* and place the *katori* in the bowl with the marinated chicken. Place a few cloves over the coal and pour one tablespoon of oil over. Immediately cover the bowl with a lid and leave to stand for a few minutes.

4 Heat the remaining oil in a *kadai*; add the onions and sauté till translucent. Add the remaining ginger paste, garlic paste and green chilli paste and sauté for two minutes.

5 Add the marinated chicken, turmeric powder, red chilli powder, coriander powder, remaining *garam masala* powder and chopped mango. Stir well so that the *masala* coats the chicken.

6 Cook on high heat for a few minutes. Add coriander leaves and a little water, cover and cook till done. Serve hot.

BUTTER CHICKEN

Ingredients

1 whole Tandoori Chicken (page 54)

Makhani Gravy

50 grams butter

1 tablespoon whole *garam masala* (green cardamoms, cloves, peppercorns and cinnamon)

1 tablespoon ginger paste

1 tablespoon garlic paste

1 teaspoon chopped green chillies

400 grams tomato purée

1 tablespoon red chilli powder

½ teaspoon *garam masala* powder

salt to taste

2 tablespoons sugar or honey

½ teaspoon dried fenugreek leaves (*kasoori methi*), crushed

1 cup fresh cream

Method

1 Shred the cooked *tandoori* chicken.

2 To make the *makhani* gravy, heat butter in a pan. Add whole *garam masala* and sauté for two minutes. Add the ginger and garlic pastes and chopped green chillies and cook for two minutes.

3 Add the tomato purée, red chilli powder, *garam masala* powder, salt and one cup of water. Bring the gravy to a boil, lower heat and simmer for ten minutes. Stir in the sugar or honey and crushed fenugreek leaves.

4 Add the *tandoori* chicken and simmer for five minutes; stir in the fresh cream.

5 Serve hot with *naans* or *paranthas.*

CHEF'S TIP

To crush dried fenugreek leaves more easily, heat them in the oven or on a tawa for a few minutes till crisp. Crush leaves between your fingers.

SHAHI MURGH KOFTA PULAO

Ingredients

- 200 grams chicken mince (*keema*)
- 1½ cups rice
- ½ teaspoon ginger, chopped
- 2 teaspoons fresh coriander leaves, chopped
- salt to taste
- 4 tablespoons oil
- 2 green cardamoms
- 1 black cardamom
- 5 cloves
- 1 bay leaf
- 1 inch cinnamon
- 2 medium onions, sliced
- ¾ teaspoon ginger paste
- 2 tablespoons tomato purée
- 1 teaspoon red chilli powder

Method

1 Wash and soak rice in three cups of water for one hour. Drain.

2 Mix together chicken mince, chopped ginger, coriander leaves and salt in a bowl. With wet hands shape small

portions of the mixture into *koftas*. Place in the refrigerator for one hour.

3 Mix oil, green cardamoms, black cardamom, cloves, bay leaf, cinnamon, onions and ginger paste in a microwave-safe bowl. Cook on HIGH (100%) for two minutes.

4 Stir in the rice and cook on HIGH (100%) for one minute.

5 Add two-and-a-half cups of water, tomato purée, salt and red chilli powder to the rice and mix well. Cook on HIGH (100%) for two minutes.

6 Add *koftas* and cover the bowl with cling wrap. Pierce the cling wrap with a few holes to let the steam escape. Cook on HIGH (100%) for seven minutes.

7 Leave to stand for five minutes and serve hot in the same bowl.

KOZHI MELAGU VARUVAL

Ingredients

1 whole chicken (800 grams), cut into 1½-inch pieces

2 tablespoons oil

5-6 garlic cloves, chopped

1 inch ginger, chopped

12-15 curry leaves

2 medium onions, chopped

1 tablespoon coriander powder

½ teaspoon turmeric powder

1 teaspoon red chilli powder

8-10 black peppercorns, crushed

3 medium tomatoes, chopped

salt to taste

2 tablespoons fresh coriander leaves, chopped

Method

1 Heat oil in a *kadai*. Add garlic, ginger, curry leaves and onions and sauté till they begin to change colour.

2 Add coriander powder, turmeric powder and red chilli powder and sauté for a few seconds. Add chicken and mix well.

3 Add freshly crushed peppercorns and sauté for five minutes.

4 Stir in the tomatoes, salt and half a cup of water.

5 Mix in the coriander leaves. Cover and cook over medium heat for about ten minutes. Serve hot.

CHEF'S TIP

This popular dish is better known as "Chettinad Chicken Pepper-Fry".

MURGH TAKA TAK

Ingredients

1 cup chicken mince (*keema*)

4 tablespoons oil

½ teaspoon cumin seeds

1 medium onion, chopped

6-7 garlic cloves, chopped

1 inch ginger, chopped

2 medium tomatoes, chopped

1 teaspoon red chilli powder

3-4 green chillies, chopped

salt to taste

2 eggs, boiled and peeled

1 teaspoon *garam masala* powder

2 tablespoons fresh coriander leaves, chopped

1 tablespoon fresh mint leaves, chopped

1 lemon

Method

1 Heat oil in a *tawa* and add cumin seeds; when they change colour, add onion and sauté for two-three minutes. Mix in the chicken mince and sauté for five minutes, breaking up mince with a metal spatula.

2 Add garlic and ginger and sauté for a few seconds. Add tomatoes, red chilli powder and green chillies and cook for a few minutes. Add a little water and cook for five more minutes.

3 Add salt and whole boiled eggs. Break the mixture up with a metal spatula.

4 Add *garam masala* powder, coriander leaves and mint leaves and mix well.

5 Sprinkle with lemon juice and serve hot directly from the *tawa.*

MAKAI MURGH

Ingredients

- 4 (150 grams each), boneless chicken breasts, skin removed
- 1 cup corn kernels, blanched
- 1 teaspoon cumin seeds
- 7-8 black peppercorns
- 1 teaspoon coriander seeds
- 5 cloves
- ½ cup yogurt
- salt to taste
- 1 teaspoon red chilli powder
- ½ teaspoon turmeric powder
- 1½ tablespoons oil
- 5-6 garlic cloves, chopped
- 1 inch ginger, chopped
- 3 medium tomatoes, puréed
- 2 medium green capsicums, cut into ½-inch cubes
- 2 tablespoons fresh coriander leaves, chopped

Method

1 Dry-roast cumin seeds, peppercorns, coriander seeds and cloves. Cool and crush coarsely.

2 Cut chicken into half-inch pieces. Place the chicken in a bowl with yogurt, salt, red chilli powder and turmeric powder and mix well.

3 Heat oil in a *kadai*; add chopped garlic and ginger and sauté for one minute. Stir in the blanched corn kernels.

4 Add half a cup of water and bring the mixture to a boil. Stir in the roasted crushed *masala*.

5 Add the fresh tomato purée and simmer for three to four minutes.

6 Add chicken, mix well and simmer till the chicken is almost done.

7 Stir in the capsicums, salt and coriander leaves and cook for one minute more.

8 Remove from heat and serve hot.

CHICKEN FARCHA

Ingredients

- 1 whole chicken (800 grams), cut into 8 pieces
- salt to taste
- 1½ tablespoons Kashmiri chilli powder
- ¾ teaspoon turmeric powder
- 1½ tablespoons ginger-garlic paste
- 2 tablespoons fresh coriander leaves, chopped
- 2 tablespoons lemon juice
- 2 eggs
- oil for deep-frying
- 1 cup breadcrumbs

Method

1 Combine salt, chilli powder, turmeric powder, ginger-garlic paste, coriander leaves and lemon juice in a bowl.

2 Add chicken pieces and mix well. Marinate chicken for at least two hours, preferably in a refrigerator.

3 Whisk eggs and salt in a bowl. Heat oil in a *kadai.*

4 Roll each piece of chicken in breadcrumbs, dip in the beaten eggs and deep-fry till golden. Drain on absorbent paper. Serve hot.

MURGH BENARASI BEEDA

Ingredients

- 250 grams boneless chicken, cut into 1-inch cubes
- ½ inch ginger, chopped
- 5 garlic cloves, chopped
- 2 green chillies
- 7-8 cashew nuts
- 8 betel leaves
- salt to taste
- 1 tablespoon lemon juice
- ½ cup drained yogurt
- ½ teaspoon *garam masala* powder
- ½ teaspoon rose water
- ½ teaspoon *kewra* water
- 2 large onions, chopped into 1-inch pieces
- 3 medium tomatoes, seeded and chopped into 1-inch pieces
- ½ tablespoon oil
- butter for basting
- onion *lachcha*
- lemon wedges

Method

1 Grind ginger, garlic and green chillies to a fine paste. Soak cashew nuts in one cup of warm water for fifteen minutes. Drain and grind to a fine paste. Wash betel leaves and make a purée of one leaf.

2 Soak wooden skewers (satay sticks) in water for at least half an hour.

3 Combine chicken, salt and lemon juice and set aside for fifteen minutes.

4 Add drained yogurt and ginger-garlic-green chilli paste to the chicken and mix well. Add betel leaf purée, cashew nut paste, *garam masala* powder, rose water, *kewra* water, onions and tomatoes and mix well. Set aside for half an hour.

5 Thread cubes of onion, chicken and tomato in that order, three times onto each skewer.

6 Heat a griddle plate. Grease with a little oil and place the skewers on it. Turn skewers and baste with butter at regular intervals.

7 Meanwhile arrange the remaining betel leaves on a serving plate. Arrange fresh *lachcha* and lemon wedges on the leaves.

8 When the chicken cubes are cooked, arrange on the betel leaves and serve hot.

CHICKEN SIZZLER WITH PEPPERS IN GARLIC SAUCE

Ingredients

- 2 (150 grams each) boneless chicken breasts, skin removed
- salt to taste
- ½ teaspoon black pepper powder
- 4½ tablespoons olive oil
- 1 medium green capsicum, cut into ½-inch pieces
- 1 medium red capsicum, cut into ½-inch pieces
- 2 fresh button mushrooms, quartered
- 3-4 cherry tomatoes
- 3-4 baby corn cobs, blanched
- 4-5 cauliflower florets, blanched
- 4-5 snow peas
- 1 medium carrot, cut into1-inch cubes, blanched
- 1 tablespoon butter
- 1 medium onion, chopped
- 4 garlic cloves, chopped
- 1 cup Brown Sauce (page 78)

oil for deep-frying

2 cups uncooked French fries

2 cabbage leaves

Method

1 Marinate chicken with salt and a quarter teaspoon of black pepper powder.

2 Heat half a tablespoon of olive oil in a pan; add the chicken and cook till tender; keep warm.

3 Heat one tablespoon of olive oil in a separate pan; sauté green and red capsicums, mushrooms, cherry tomatoes, baby corn, cauliflower, snow peas and carrot with salt and remaining black pepper powder. Set aside.

4 For the garlic sauce, heat one tablespoon of butter; add onion and garlic and sauté for a few seconds. Stir in the brown sauce and adjust seasonings.

5 Heat oil in a deep pan and deep-fry French fries till golden. Drain on absorbent paper.

6 Heat a sizzler plate and place it on its wooden base. Arrange cabbage leaves on the plate. Arrange the cooked chicken breasts, sautéed vegetables and French fries on the cabbage leaves.

7 Pour the prepared sauce over the chicken and serve immediately.

BROWN SAUCE

Boil 250 grams of mutton bones with 1 chopped onion, 1 chopped celery stalk, 2 chopped tomatoes, 3 black peppercorns and 1 bay leaf with enough water to cover for about one hour. Strain.

Melt 2 tablespoons of butter in a pan; add 2 tablespoons of flour and cook over low heat till brown. Stir in 1 cup of mutton stock, add salt and black pepper to taste. Cook for 10 minutes, stirring continuously. Strain.

CHICKEN STEW WITH GARLIC BREAD

Ingredients

- 500 grams chicken, cut into 1½-inch cubes
- 1½ tablespoons unsalted butter
- ½ tablespoon garlic, sliced
- 1 medium onion, sliced fine
- 1 medium carrot, cubed
- 1 medium potato, peeled and cubed
- 1½ tablespoons wholewheat flour (*atta*)
- salt to taste
- 2½ cups Chicken Stock (page 10)
- ¼ teaspoon black pepper powder
- 3-4 French beans, cut into 1-inch pieces
- ¼ cup milk

Garlic Bread

- 1 French loaf
- 4 tablespoons salted butter
- 2 teaspoons garlic paste
- ½ teaspoon black peppercorns, crushed

Method

1 Heat butter in a pan; add garlic, onion, carrot and potato and sauté for four to five minutes on high heat till all the moisture dries up.

2 Add wholewheat flour to the vegetables and sauté for one minute. Add chicken and salt and sauté for eight to ten minutes.

3 Add chicken stock and bring the mixture to a boil. Stir in half the black pepper powder, cover and cook for three to four minutes.

4 Add French beans and cook till done.

5 Stir in the milk and the remaining black pepper powder. Cover and cook on medium heat for seven to eight minutes.

6 To make the garlic bread, preheat the oven to 200°C.

7 Cream salted butter till smooth, add garlic paste and crushed black peppercorns.

8 Slice the French loaf diagonally two inches apart, without cutting through; spread butter generously between the slices. Wrap the whole loaf in aluminium foil and cook in the oven for five to eight minutes.

9 Serve the chicken stew with hot garlic bread.

CHICKEN LAKSA

Ingredients

- 500 grams boneless chicken, cut into thin strips
- 1 inch fresh ginger
- 3-4 garlic cloves
- 4 shallots
- 2 lemon grass stalks
- 3 tablespoons sesame oil
- 3 cups Chicken Stock (page 10)
- 2 fresh red chillies, seeded and sliced
- 1 teaspoon curry powder
- 100 grams snow peas
- salt to taste
- pepper powder to taste
- 1 tablespoon lemon juice
- ½ cup coconut milk

To Serve

- 1 cup boiled noodles
- 2-3 spring onions, finely sliced
- 1 medium unpeeled cucumber, sliced
- 1 tablespoon fresh coriander leaves, chopped
- 1 tablespoon fresh mint leaves, chopped
- 2 lemons, halved

Method

1 Grind ginger, garlic, shallots and lemon grass to a paste.

2 Heat two tablespoons of sesame oil in a large frying-pan or wok and cook the chicken over high heat until golden. Drain on absorbent paper.

3 In the same pan, heat the remaining oil; add the ground paste and sauté for a few minutes.

4 Stir in the chicken stock, red chillies, curry powder, snow peas, salt and pepper powder.

5 Add lemon juice and coconut milk and bring the mixture to a boil.

6 To serve, place boiled noodles in serving bowls, add chicken, spring onions, cucumber, coriander and mint leaves.

7 Pour hot soup into the bowls; fix half a lemon onto the rim of each bowl and serve immediately.

SPAGHETTI WITH CHICKEN AND EGGPLANTS

Ingredients

- 100 grams spaghetti
- 2 (150 grams each) boneless chicken breasts
- 4-5 small eggplants (brinjals)
- salt to taste
- 6 tablespoons oil
- 1 tablespoon mustard paste
- 3 medium tomatoes
- 2 green capsicums, cut into thin strips
- 3-4 garlic cloves, chopped
- ¼ cup tomato ketchup
- 5-6 black peppercorns, crushed
- 1 teaspoon crushed red chillies
- 3 tablespoons fresh parsley, finely chopped
- 1 teaspoon butter
- ¾ cup grated cheese

Method

1 In a large pan, boil spaghetti in three cups of salted water with one tablespoon of oil, till nearly cooked (al dente). Drain, stir in one tablespoon of oil and spread on a plate to cool.

2 Pat the chicken dry and cut into quarter-inch by one-and-a-half-inch long strips. Marinate the chicken in mustard paste for about fifteen to twenty minutes.

3 Cut eggplants into thin round slices and soak in cold salted water for ten minutes. Drain and pat dry.

4 Blanch tomatoes in two cups of boiling water for two to three minutes. Peel, remove seeds and chop roughly to make tomato concasse.

5 Preheat oven to 160°C.

6 Heat two tablespoons of oil in a frying-pan and sauté the chicken. Stir in the capsicum strips.

7 Heat one tablespoon of oil in a separate frying-pan; add garlic and sauté for a few seconds. Add tomato concasse and tomato ketchup and mix well. Add salt, one-third of the crushed black peppercorns and one tablespoon of chopped parsley.

8 Gently, but thoroughly, mix cooked spaghetti into the sauce. Remove from heat and set aside.

9 Heat the remaining oil in a separate frying-pan; add eggplant and cook on low heat. Stir in salt, one-third of the peppercorns, half a teaspoon of crushed red chillies and half a tablespoon of parsley. Turn the slices over and season with salt, remaining peppercorns, remaining crushed red chillies and half a tablespoon of parsley.

10 Grease the base and sides of a baking dish with butter. Arrange the cooked chicken and capsicum at the bottom of the dish. Spread spaghetti over the chicken.

11 Cover the spaghetti with the eggplant. Sprinkle grated cheese and the remaining chopped parsley over the eggplant.

12 Cook in the preheated oven for ten to fifteen minutes and serve hot.

HERB-CRUSTED CHICKEN WITH PEACH SAUCE

Ingredients

- 4 (150 grams each) boneless chicken breasts, skin removed
- ½ cup fresh parsley, puréed
- 4 fresh peaches, peeled, stoned and puréed
- ½ cup refined flour (*maida*)
- salt to taste
- black pepper powder to taste
- 5 tablespoons olive oil (preferably garlic-flavoured)
- 1 tablespoon butter
- ½ cup red wine
- ½ cup fresh breadcrumbs
- 1 medium red capsicum, diced
- 1 medium yellow capsicum, diced
- 1 medium green capsicum, diced
- 3-4 garlic cloves, chopped
- fresh parsley, to garnish

Method

1 Mix *maida,* salt and black pepper powder in a plate. Roll chicken breasts in the mixture and set aside.

2 Heat two tablespoons of olive oil in a pan. Shallow-fry chicken breasts on medium heat, turning over once to brown evenly.

3 Heat butter in a separate pan. Add red wine and peach purée and cook for five minutes till thick. Set aside.

4 Preheat the oven to 200°C. Grease a baking tray and arrange fried chicken breasts in it.

5 Spread parsley purée thickly over the chicken breasts and drizzle with one tablespoon of olive oil.

6 Sprinkle breadcrumbs, salt, black pepper powder and one more tablespoon of olive oil over the chicken. Bake the chicken for ten minutes.

7 Pour the remaining olive oil into the pan in which the chicken has been fried. Add the capsicums and sauté for two to three minutes. Stir in the garlic, salt and black pepper powder.

8 Arrange chicken on a serving platter. Pour peach sauce on one side and arrange capsicums on the other. Serve hot, garnished with sprigs of parsley.

STUFFED ROAST CHICKEN

Ingredients

- 1 whole chicken (1 kilogram)
- salt to taste
- 4 tablespoons butter

Stuffing

- 3 tablespoons oil
- 2 medium onions, chopped
- 5-6 fresh button mushrooms, chopped
- 1 medium pear, peeled and grated
- 1 medium apple, peeled and grated
- 2 chicken livers, chopped
- salt to taste
- ½ teaspoon black pepper powder
- 6-8 cashew nuts, chopped
- 2 tablespoons chopped walnuts
- ½ cup breadcrumbs
- ½ cup milk
- 2 eggs, lightly beaten
- butter or oil for basting

Method

1 Leave the skin on the chicken. Remove neck, wash the chicken thoroughly and wipe dry. Apply salt all over the chicken, including inside the cavity.

2 Preheat the oven to 200°C.

3 For the stuffing, heat the oil in a pan; add onions and mushrooms and stir-fry for a few seconds. Add the pear and apple and sauté for a few seconds.

4 Add the chicken liver, salt, half the black pepper powder, cashew nuts and walnuts and sauté for a while.

5 Place the breadcrumbs in a bowl and stir in the milk, beaten eggs, remaining black pepper powder and salt to taste. Add to the cooked mixture and mix well.

6 Spoon the stuffing inside the chicken and press lightly. Tie up the legs and fold in the wings.

7 Place the stuffed chicken on a rack over a roasting pan, and cook in the oven for thirty to forty minutes till golden brown. Baste with butter or oil two or three times while cooking.

8 Remove from the oven and leave to cool slightly before carving into slices.

FRIED CHICKEN WINGS WITH CHILLI-PINEAPPLE SAUCE

Ingredients

16 chicken wings
2 pineapple slices, finely chopped
3 garlic cloves, chopped
1 tablespoon brown sugar
2 tablespoons soy sauce
4-5 black peppercorns, crushed
2 fresh red chillies, sliced
1 tablespoon lemon juice
salt to taste
1 tablespoon tamarind pulp
3 tablespoons oil
2 tablespoons pineapple juice

Chilli-Pineapple Sauce

5-6 pineapple slices, puréed
1 cup pineapple juice
1 tablespoon brown sugar
salt to taste
1 tablespoon cornflour
2 fresh red chillies, sliced

Method

1 Clean, wash and trim chicken wings. Soak wooden satay sticks in water for at least 15 minutes.

2 In a blender, process chopped pineapple, garlic, brown sugar, soy sauce, crushed black peppercorns, fresh red chillies, lemon juice and salt till smooth.

3 Add tamarind pulp and one tablespoon of oil and mix well. Marinate the chicken wings in the mixture for three hours.

4 Thread the marinated wings onto the satay sticks.

5 Heat a *tawa* and add the oil. Place the skewered chicken wings on the *tawa* and cook on high heat for three to five minutes. Turn over to cook the other side.

6 Lower heat, add pineapple juice and cook till nicely browned.

7 For the sauce, place the pineapple purée, pineapple juice, brown sugar and salt in a pan and mix well.

8 Bring the mixture to a boil; add cornflour mixed with three tablespoons of water. Stir well and add the red chillies. Cook on low heat, stirring continuously, till the sauce thickens.

9 Serve with the fried chicken wings.

KUNG PAO CHICKEN

Ingredients

- 400 grams boneless chicken breasts
- salt to taste
- 3 tablespoons soy sauce
- ¼ teaspoon MSG (optional)
- ½ teaspoon white pepper powder
- 2 tablespoons lemon juice
- 3-4 spring onions, chopped
- 5-6 dried red chillies, broken in half
- 4-5 garlic cloves, chopped
- 1 inch ginger, chopped
- 1½ cups Chicken Stock (page 10)
- 2 teaspoons sugar
- 2 tablespoons cornflour
- ¼ cup roasted peanuts
- 1 stalk spring onion greens, chopped

Method

1 Cut chicken into one-inch pieces. Add salt, two tablespoons of soy sauce, MSG, white pepper powder and one tablespoon of lemon juice and mix well.

2 Heat a wok; add spring onions, red chillies, garlic and ginger and cook for two to three minutes. Add a little water to prevent the onions from browning.

3 Add the marinated chicken and chicken stock and cook till the chicken is tender.

4 Add the remaining soy sauce, sugar and cornflour mixed with half a cup of water. Stir in the roasted peanuts.

5 Add the chopped spring onion greens and the remaining lemon juice and serve hot.